My Blended

Written by

Emma Lee Picone

And a little help from my mom
Amy Oberg

Illustrated by

Tina Harrel

Joshua Tree Publishing
• Chicago •

JoshuaTreePublishing.com

ISBN: 978-0-9829803-9-2

Printed in the United States of America

Hi my name is Emma Lee, and I live in a blended family.

A blended
family is...

where I live at
My Mom's house
and My Dad's house.

Even though
They don't live together.

kind,
gentle,
caring,
cool,
playful, and happy.

I HAVE lots of
family too!

I HAVE A
mom, dad,
step parents,
aunts, uncles,
cousins,
grandmas,
grandpas,
great
grandparents

and
animals on every
side.

Some kids even
have
half brothers and
half sisters or
step brothers and
step sisters.

When I was little,
I used to call each night a
nap.
I would say I'm going to
stay
3 naps at Moms
or 3 naps Dads.

Monday

Sunday

Tuesday

But now..
I know the days
of the week

Saturday

Wednesday

Friday

Thursday

Sometimes it was easier.. by saying what days I will be gone ... or helping mom or dad get my stuff ready to go.

We have tried
many different
schedules...
and so have some
of my friends that
go back and forth.

I go back and
forth every couple
of days.
Sometimes it's
okay...
and sometimes...
it's kind of
annoying.

Every once in a while
I would get
confused on my
days
and I would get
sad.

But I would remember that...

I could call the other parent to say hello and...
I miss you and...
I love you.

Sometimes I would get scared when I woke up in the middle of the night because, I didn't know if I was at Moms or Dads.

It helped me
to have
a special
stuffed
animal and
a special
night light
at each
house.

I have 2 rooms, 2 beds, 2 houses, 2 closets,
2 kitchens, 2 sets of animals
lots of shoes,
and lots of clothes.

I think it's pretty cool that
I get 1 holiday at each house.
That means that I get...2 birthdays,
2 Thanksgivings and 2 Christmases.

I must be pretty
special!!
They must
really love me!!

Sometimes I'm sad because...
I miss the other Parent

They miss me too!!

They say...
Even though I'm there
only half the time...

They both love me 100% of the time.

They say that it's hard to
not see me everyday.

And it's also very hard for me
to be with only one parent and
not the other.

Sometimes....
When I'm at my Mom's house
I want to be at my Dad's house.
And When I'm at my Dad's house...
I want to be at Mom's house.

Sometimes...

it's just

HARD!!

One time it got
really HARD
and I talked to
someone who wasn't in
Mom's family
or Dad's family.

She was a special person
called a counselor.
And she helped me be
HAPPY
at both of my homes!
YAY!!!

It will ALWAYS be important to me that I have BOTH parents in my life.

Because
I love them
100%
of the time
too.

Even though it's hard sometimes,
I follow the rules
and always tell the truth.

Because the truth is
always the same, just like me!!

I'm the same person
At my Mom's and my Dad's house.
I get to be the same person
No matter where I go.

I'm smart, funny,
loving, caring,
helpful, exciting,
talented, adventurous,
and...

I am a
One-of-a-kind
GREAT KID!!
Just like
YOU!

It's not the
end...
it's just the
beginning of
my life.

And yours!

I know what I'm doing. I have it all
planned out
plans to take care of you,
not abandon you,
plans to give you the future you hope for.
Jeremiah 29:11

Be strong and courageous, do not be
terrified,
do not be discouraged,
for the Lord your God will be with you
wherever you go.
Joshua 1:9

CPSIA information can be obtained
at www.ICGtesting.com
Printed in the USA
436574LV00004B/27